Praying the Promises of the Cross

40-DAY PRAYER JOURNAL

ARABAH JOY & AMANDA CRISS

Arabah Joy LLC

By Arabah Joy and Amanda Criss

Praying the Promises of the Cross - 40 Day Prayer Journal by Arabah Joy and Amanda Criss

ISBN-13: 978-0692868652
ISBN-10: 0692868658

Contents

How This Little Ol' Journal Came to Be

The book of Joshua is all about inheritances. Which may be why I like it so much.

Each Israelite tribe (excluding the tribe of Levi, for the Lord was their portion) was given land to take possession of. Much like you'd take possession of a bank account left to you in a will or a gun collection passed to you from a relative, the Israelites were to go into the Promised Land and take it over.

Yet some of the tribes failed to fully possess their inheritance. Some put off strapping on their swords and doing the hard work of settling an untamed, enemy infested land.

It's understandable. I imagine it would be like loading up the car and heading down to Florida where a pearl necklace passed down from your grandmother awaits you. You know it's a nice piece of jewelry but you also know it's going to cost several hundred dollars to get down there, not to mention time away from work and the trouble of getting the family on board with the plan. Plus, you've got a mean cousin who's currently in possession of that necklace and she's promised to fight you for it.

Turns out, the Israelites weren't so keen on duking it out with the Canaanites either. But Joshua knew the inheritance that awaited God's people far exceeded the costs and inconveniences involved in possessing it. So Joshua, in chapter 18 verse 3, said to them, "How long will you put off entering to take possession of the land which the Lord, the God of your fathers, has given you?"

Joshua called them on their complacency... their comfort... their status quo... and challenged them to move into a place of possessing promises. The Promised Land had been given to them and it was a good gift!

Joshua then instructed them to, "Choose three men to get up and walk through the land. Have them write a description of it according to their inheritance."

If you are like me, right about now you are saying, "Wait a minute. Why did Joshua tell them to do that? What's the big deal about sending some men to go look at the land and write some details down? Why didn't he just tell them to get to possessing it already?"

It's a good question...and a telling one. I think it's because the people needed to know the goodness, richness, and wealth they were missing out on. They needed a fire in their bones to suit up and head out. I mean, if you were told your poor old grandma left you that necklace and some money in the bank but you'd have to duke out a legal battle with that mean cousin to get it, you might drag your feet.

But if you were told your poor old grandma left you a necklace and some money in the bank to the surprising sum of a 1 followed by seven zeros (see, like my fancy description?) you might be ready to go at it with that cousin of yours.

After all, the necklace and money is yours...and it's worth the headache of getting it into your possession.

It's the same for us spiritually. We have an immensely valuable inheritance in Christ. But how often do we put off truly taking possession of the wealth God has provided us? Possessing promises is hard work. It takes effort. It tests our determination, faith, our brainpower, and our brawn. It's much easier to become complacent, settling for amusements, gadgets and distractions. In doing so, however, we miss out on the rich inheritance provided us in Christ.

Joshua knew the Israelites needed motivation to move out of their complacency. He knew they would never possess the land God had given them if they didn't have something to light their fire. He knew a deeper under-

standing of their inheritance was just the fire they needed.

And sometimes, it's what we need too. Having rich descriptions of our promises written down becomes vital to
our success and having a systematic way of reminding
ourselves of truth gives us a battle plan.

This isn't some silly gun collection we are talking here; it
isn't grandma's pearl necklace. It's the inheritance of
"every spiritual blessing in the heavenly places in Christ
Jesus." (see Ephesians 1:3)

If that fails to motivate you, perhaps it's because you need
some timely descriptions regarding your inheritance. You
need to see the number of zeros after the one. You need a
few details filled in that will ignite your fire and motivate
you to high tail it down to the attorney's office to sign
those ownership papers.

Which brings us to the point. We have such a magnifi-
cent spiritual inheritance in Christ. It is much more valuable than gold, land, or someone's stamp collection. Our
inheritance is so priceless it had to be purchased on our
behalf with the very blood of our God and King, Jesus
Christ.

Yes, brothers and sister, we have obtained an inheritance. But we can sit complacent and comfortable. We
can stay entertained by the world's amusements and put

off taking possession of the wealth we've been given. Maybe, just maybe, we need others in our midst to walk the length of the land and write descriptions of our inheritance so we can get fired up and get busy claiming it.

Joshua 18 reports that men arose who walked through the land. They described it in seven divisions in a book, a book that became instrumental in moving the Israelites to action. These descriptions compelled the Israelites to divide the inheritance and take possession of it.

Perhaps we too could use a jumpstart to our spiritual motors. Perhaps we need to awaken afresh to the wealth of the gospel. Maybe you need to move beyond mediocrity. The aim of this journal is to start your engine anew, all cylinders go, for possessing your spiritual inheritance.

Regarding those ancient ones who failed to possess their promises, the writer of Hebrews said, "For this reason (because it is easy to put off possessing promises), we must pay much closer attention to what we have heard, so that we do not drift away from it. For how shall we escape if we neglect so great a salvation?" (Hebrews 2:1,3)

Let it not be said of us that we missed out on what God had for us, that we neglected so great a salvation, so rich an inheritance, so wide a possession! Instead, let us stir one another on to faith and rouse one another to action. Our inheritance is much too precious to neglect.

My prayer is that the eyes of our hearts be enlightened, that we would know the hope of His calling and the riches of His inheritance in us, the saints. (Ephesians 1:18) May this little journal be used to that end.

Arabah Joy

www.arabahjoy.com

The Transforming Power of the Gospel

*"Like newborn babies, long for the pure milk of the word,
so that by it you may grow in respect to salvation."*
- I Peter 2:2

For many years, I had the erroneous idea that the gospel
was important good news for those who didn't know
Christ, but after being saved, Christians needed to move
on past the gospel in their spiritual growth. I saw the
gospel more like a "point A" starting place for spiritual
growth rather than the foundation of our entire Christian life.

Rather than the gospel being one of many important bib-
lical truths, the gospel is the good news of salvation
through Jesus Christ. Christians can't "grow past" the
gospel as they progress in faith by God's grace; rather, the
gospel is the truth and means by which Christians grow
up in every way into Him who is the Head, into Christ.
By it we become mature and learn to walk worthy of our
Master, King Jesus.

Paul says in 1 Corinthians 15 that those who've believed in Jesus stand in this saving gospel. Staying tethered to the gospel does not mean our faith is stagnant! Growing in the gospel means that we grow in our knowledge and in the grace of Jesus Christ our Savior, always clinging to the cross, always clinging to His righteousness, and always worshiping our Savior, the Lamb who was slain for our sins even before the foundation of the world.

Over the last few weeks, as I have been writing entries for this journal, my heart has been filled to overflowing with confidence, joy, and hope in our Savior and Redeemer. I have been reminded of Who He is, what He has done, and what He will do. I am also reminded of who I am, what I have done, and what He has promised to do for me. This season of soaking and basking in the gospel has been immensely rich and has strengthened my heart and grown my love for my Beloved, the precious Savior of the world, Jesus Christ.

My hope for you as you study these 40 Scripture texts is that you will know Jesus, believe Jesus and love Jesus. If you have never trusted in Jesus for the forgiveness of your sins, believe on Him today. If you are unsure whether or not He has ever saved you from your sins and the coming judgment, believe His word and claim only the righteousness of Christ as you cry out to the Father. If your heart thrills at the sound of the good news that has saved your soul, go deeper in the gospel and grow in respect to your salvation.

May God grant you to find unspeakable joy in the sacrifice of His Son on your behalf, and may He strengthen your heart as you consider the risen Savior. I hope this journal is like dipping your toes into a cool oasis in the heat of summer. May this little taste of milk from the Word of God so whet your appetite for Jesus that you dive headlong and go down deeper and deeper into Jesus through His word. He is our life, and the Scriptures testify of Him.

Don't stay spiritually dehydrated, only sipping occasionally from the Word of God. The good news of the Bible is not an idle word; it is your very life. Grow in respect to your salvation by drinking deeply from the Word of God. Hear, obey, and remember the gospel of God's Word, and may the One you find there quench your thirst so out of your heart will flow rivers of living water. As you grow in your knowledge and understanding of the sacrifice of the Son of God on your behalf, may your soul sing, "This is my Beloved, and this is my Friend."

Amanda Criss
www.blessyourheartandhome.com

How to Use this Journal

To help you get the most out of your 40-day prayer jour-
ney, you will find a few aids on the journal pages that follow.

Read It: This section will give you the passage for each
day. Always begin by reading the verse in your Bible. If
you have the time, look the verse up in several different
versions to get a robust understanding of the scripture's
intent.

Write It: While this section is for writing the daily passage out, you can also use it to articulate the day's promise in your own words. Sometimes thinking through the
passage and putting it in your own words facilitates a
deeper understanding of the verse.

Ponder It: In this section you'll find a brief journal entry
from either Arabah (AJ) or Amanda (AC). We've included these thoughts as supplementary reading, as if we
were discussing our thoughts on the passage with you
over coffee. These snippets are intended to stimulate and

encourage your gospel thinking. They are not replacements for the Scripture itself.

Pray It: Here is where you will exercise your faith. Using the scripture and insights gained while meditating as prompts, pray the passage back to God. You may begin by re-stating the verse, acknowledging the specific things Christ has done on your behalf, and asking God for faith to believe this is yours in Christ. Voice your "amen" to God's promise in accordance with II Corinthians 1:20 (see more details on this here: www.arabahjoy.com/40-promises). Thank the Lord for His gift and ask for a deeper understanding of the riches you have been given. You will find that putting this all down on paper will force you to meditate on and articulate truth in deeper ways... and, with surprising results.

As we have prepared this journal for you, we've spent many hours reading, meditating on, and journaling about the scriptures here. We can both say it has been one of the richest, most rewarding times of our lives. We pray the next 40 days is the same for you.

Now strap on your sandals. Let's go take some promises. In Him and For Him, Arabah Joy from www.arabahjoy.-com and Amanda Criss from www.blessyourheartand-home.com

PRAYING THE PROMISES OF THE CROSS
QUICK REFERENCE GUIDE

Day One: John 3:16
Day Two: Romans 8:32
Day Three: Romans 4:20, 22-25
Day Four: 2 Corinthians 5:17-18
Day Five: Hebrews 10:19,22
Day Six: Colossians 2:13-14
Day Seven: Romans 4:7-8
Day Eight: II Corinthians 5:21
Day Nine: Titus 2:14
Day Ten: Romans 8:1
Day Eleven: Ephesians 2:12-13
Day Twelve: Hebrews 2:14-15
Day Thirteen: I Corinthians 1:30-31
Day Fourteen: Titus 3:5
Day Fifteen: I Peter 1:18-19
Day Sixteen: Romans 8:10-11
Day Seventeen: I John 4:10
Day Eighteen: Romans 5:12-21
Day Nineteen: Romans 6:11-13
Day Twenty: Ephesians 2:4-5, Romans 6:11
Day Twenty-One: I Timothy 1:15
Day Twenty-Two: Romans 5:1
Day Twenty-Three: Hebrews 9:14
Day Twenty-Four: I Peter 1:3-4
Day Twenty-Five: II Corinthians 3:18
Day Twenty-Six: Romans 15:7
Day Twenty-Seven: Romans 8:33-34

READ IT

Day One: John 3:16

Write it:

_____

_____

_____

_____

_____

Ponder it:

Like a careening planet in some sci-fi movie, Earth and everything on it is headed for destruction. But God loved, so God gave. God provided a way of escape. God isn't some jovial Santa Claus, doling out health, wealth, and prosperity to those who believe enough or think positive enough. God is the King of the Universe, holding all knowledge, all power and all sovereignty, who loves us enough to stoop low and enter the womb of a woman so that He could die on our behalf. The promise of the cross starts here, with God's love. This love is so deep it does what's best for us, even when the cost was

His one and only Son. This love will always go the distance. It already has. AJ

Pray it:

READ IT

Day Two: Romans 8:32

Write it:

Ponder it:

The Father did not spare His only begotten Son, the One whom He loved, the One with Whom He was pleased, and the One who lived perfectly in our stead. If God was pleased to crush Jesus to bear our sin, then we understand He has already done the hardest, greatest, most marvelous work on our behalf. We see that painful, terribly glorious sacrifice on the cross, and we are left with no room for doubts or fears that He will not also through His Son freely lavish on us all things pertaining to life and godliness that culminate in our promised glorification with Him. Through our present sufferings and in our earthly groanings, we cling to the love of God in Christ Jesus, living this life with a steadfast hope and expectant joy in the sure promises of God that await us. AC

Pray it:

READ IT

Day Three: Romans 4:20, 22-25

Write it:

_____

_____

_____

_____

_____

Ponder it:

For my sake these things are written, so that I might confidently know God is satisfied. Righteousness has been credited to me. Like a million dollars being credited to my bank account as a gift from one of the world's richest men, perfect righteousness is credited to me. What's the proof of this amazing claim? The resurrection of Christ. Christ's resurrection is proof of an essential spiritual reality that I get to be the beneficiary of: God is satisfied with Christ's work. He is pleased. He accepted the work of Christ on my behalf and I am right with Him. Put into every day terms, God has no beef with me. Praise the Lord for His indescribable gift! AJ

Pray it:

READ IT

Day Four: 2 Corinthians 5:17-18

Write it:

_____

_____

_____

_____

_____

Ponder it:

We don't come to Jesus simply for a do-over. When by grace through faith we are born again, the gift we receive is not just a clean slate, but we very literally become a new man or woman. Our old self is crucified with Him, in order that our body of sin might be done away with, so that we would no longer be slaves to sin, but alive to God in Christ Jesus. Our searching and scrambling for a new start is not fulfilled in turning over a new leaf, but in becoming a new creation by the power of our Creator God who said, "Light shall shine out of darkness." This darkness-penetrating God, who is the One who shone in our hearts to give the Light of the knowledge of the glory of God in the face of Christ, commissions His newly created vessels to call to a blind and stumbling world, "We beg you on behalf of Christ, be reconciled to God!" And because the calling, creating, and saving are all of God, we fulfill our ministry in total dependence upon Him, knowing that the surpassing greatness of the power is of God and not from ourselves. AC

Pray it:

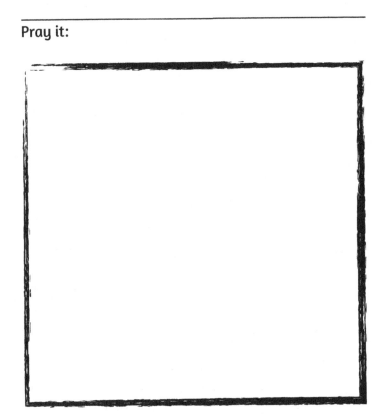

READ IT

Day Five: Hebrews 10:19

Write it:

_____

_____

_____

_____

_____

Ponder it:

The blood of Christ purchased confidence for me. For one who struggles with insecurity and a deep sense of her own ineptness, this is good news to be sure. If I can have confidence to enter the Holy Place, the throne room of the Most High God, should I lack confidence to live out any of my days here on earth? Soul, what is shaking your confidence? Your sin? Your imperfection? It was for these that Christ died! What is shaking your confidence? The opinion of others? Your pride? Christ's blood has overcome whatever that "thing" is. The voice of insecurity lies; it must submit to the Lordship of Christ. Draw

near in full assurance of faith, for Jesus Christ has purchased the solid ground on which you stand. AJ

Pray it:

READ IT

Day Six: Colossians 2:13-14

Write it:

_____

_____

_____

_____

_____

Ponder it:

Although the Jews debated with Pilate about the record of crimes to be nailed to the cross of Jesus, the crucifixion onlookers didn't realize it was their own personal records of debt that were the crimes for which Jesus suffered. We see our names written on a placard, filled to overflowing with a record of all our sin and crimes against God. Our placard of shame is nailed atop Jesus' cross, and then He hangs there, suffering and dying for our sins, for our crimes against God. But as He breathes His last, He utters, "IT IS FINISHED," and God stamps in red across the certificate of debt belonging to believing souls: "PAID IN

FULL." The debt is cancelled, our shame is over, and all of our sin has been forgiven. Hallelujah! AC

Pray it:

READ IT

Day Seven: Romans 4:7-8

Write it:

_____

_____

_____

_____

_____

Ponder it:

Acquitted. This legal term means little to the innocent, but to the person guilty of capital offense, it becomes the pursuit of their lives. The law's arm of justice operates as the avenger, administering just punishment for sin. God's perfect holiness brings perfect justice... which means not even the slightest sin is overlooked. All are duly noted and we stand before a Holy God without hope. Our record of wrongdoing is long, the outcome of our court appearing is bleak. But just as God provided cities of refuge in the Old Testament, He provided a refuge for us, a safe place from the avenger of blood. The perfect Judge who administers justice and cannot tolerate sin, has also made a way for us to be acquitted. Acquitted! "To be found not guilty of a criminal offense; legally blameless." That's the promise of Christ's work on the cross. AJ

Pray it:

READ IT

Day Eight: 2 Corinthians 5:21

Write it:

_____

_____

_____

_____

_____

Ponder it:

And here is the most unfair verse in all of Scripture. Perfect God becomes a perfect man who lives a perfect life, and then not only dies for our sin, but God the Father makes God the Son to BE sin on our behalf, so that all of God's righteous wrath against sinners could be poured out and quenched by taking vengeance against sin on His only Son. Why did God do this? So that you and I, imperfect sinners by our very nature and in our deeds, might BECOME the righteousness of God. God's wrath is satisfied through the Son that He punished on our behalf, and for any soul who trusts in Jesus for the forgive-

ness of their sin, God offers them reconciliation and forgiveness. We are offered God's pardon because the list of
all our grievances against God was hammered to Jesus'
cross. And we are offered Jesus' perfect record of obedi-
ence because His life embodied perfection, and God im-
putes the righteousness of Jesus to the account of forgiv-
en sinners for whom He gave His only begotten Son. AC

Pray it:

READ IT

Day Nine: Titus 2:14

Write it:

_____

_____

_____

_____

_____

Ponder it:

Some days I wake with no desire for God, no hunger for the holy. I'm content to please myself and I'm happy to remain lukewarm and mediocre. My affections are not stirred to godliness and I wonder how to kindle a fire for the things of God. Into this pathetic state Titus 2 speaks. God has never expected me to come up with my own righteousness, not even in the form of godly desire, and never will. I'm totally dependent upon Him for that... and He is pleased when I trust Him for it and allow His grace to be what feeds and nurtures godly desire. Christ's work purchased my purification, the cleansing of my heart, will and desires. His work entitles me a zeal for good deeds! When my desires do not align themselves with the holy and righteous things of God, I can approach the throne room and plead the blood of Jesus. I ask for my inheritance. Christ has purchased a zealous heart, one eager for goodness, quickened to holiness, and hungry for righteousness. AJ

Pray it:

READ IT

Day Ten: Romans 8:1

Write it:

Ponder it:

"No guilt in life, no fear in death -- this is the pow'r of Christ in me." Our hearts can scarcely fathom that the words from this beautiful hymn could be true. No guilt? But we are guilty! No fear? But we are worthy of pun-ishment. Oh, but since Jesus came in the likeness of sinful flesh, and since He was our offering for sin, it is sin that is now condemned, and not the sinner. And since we lay claim to the righteousness of Jesus, it is His perfectly lived life and sacrificial death that satisfy God's righteous requirement of perfection. Our record of punishment-worthy trespasses against a holy God has been nailed to the cross of His Son. The only One worthy to bring a charge against you is God the Father, and He it is who justifies you through His Son! The One worthy to condemn you is the Son who died for you, and He it is who lives forever to intercede for you before the Father. Your heart is free to bask in the love of God for you, for Jesus bore all your guilt and condemnation and as a result of the anguish of His soul, God is satisfied. AC

Pray it:

READ IT

Day Eleven: Ephesians 2:12-13

Write it:

_____

_____

_____

_____

_____

Ponder it:

Left out in the cold. Have you ever experienced that? Perhaps you are experiencing deep rejection, isolation, and hopelessness right now. Scripture tells us to remember what it's like to be the castaway- for in order for our hearts to be thrilled by the gospel, pulsating with joy, we need to recall what it was like to be separated from Christ. Excluded. Strangers. The one who doesn't belong and who isn't welcomed. But Christ changed all that! His blood gave us a brand new identity, casting us in a whole new light. We who were formerly the outsiders are now "brought near." We are transferred to a new kingdom. If you are in Christ, you are brought near to God. No longer the outsider, no longer the "nobody." You are included. Accepted. Beneficiary. Royalty. AJ

Pray it:

READ IT

Day Twelve: Hebrews 2:14-15

Write it:

_____

_____

_____

_____

_____

Ponder it:

In a black dress and heels, I watch my grandfather's cas-
ket being lowered into the earth. I find great comfort in
hearing the words of Paul from 1 Corinthians 15 read,
promises of resurrection, freedom, and victory. That
godly old man, a soul who clung to the righteousness of
Jesus for decade after decade after decade, has reaped
immortality, life, and heaven. As I stand there, heart
aching and soul quivering, I feel a strange boldness as I
hear the taunt, "O death, where is your victory? O death,
where is your sting?" For Jesus, the Savior and Overcom-
er to Whom my grandfather had entrusted his soul, also

once took residence in a body, tasted death for every man, and became the first to be resurrected from the dead. Someday, my grandfather and all who are in Christ will follow in bodily resurrection with the One who made propitiation for our sins, death and the devil will be destroyed, and we will forever taste the victory that God gives us through His Son, Jesus Christ. AC

Pray it:

READ IT

Day Thirteen: 1 Corinthians 1:30–31

Write it:

_____

_____

_____

_____

_____

Ponder it:

"By His doing." Wisdom, righteousness, sanctification and redemption are ours by His doing. When faced with our great lack and insufficiency of these things, we can either turn to various means of producing, creating, faking, or gaining them (or give up altogether); or we can rest in the promise of the cross. "By His doing you are in Christ, who became all these things to me." Though I am sinful and weak, lacking in smarts and charismatic appeal, I'm the very type God chooses, in order that His name would receive the glory. By His doing we are equipped, so let us adorn ourselves with the gospel and let us boast in the Lord. Yes, let us exult in Christ! AJ

Pray it:

READ IT

Day Fourteen: Titus 3:5

Write it:

_____

_____

_____

_____

_____

Ponder it:

Washed and renewed: these two aspects of our new birth into Christ are good news for our needy souls. In God's great mercy, filthy sinners are purged clean by the blood of the One who removes soul stains, by the One who cries out, "Come now, let us reason together...though your sins are like scarlet, they shall be as white as snow..." We cannot earn this change by any goodness of our own, but we are simply on the receiving end of the goodness, loving kindness, and mercy of God our Savior who justifies us by His grace. He not only scrubs white the scarlet letter painted over the sinner's heart, but He renews the sinner, so that by the Spirit of Jesus we are born again. In our new birth, our redeemed souls pant for the total renewal and redemption that awaits us who are now heirs according to the hope of eternal life. Our renewed spirits are first-fruits; they are a precious taste of the immeasurable riches of God's grace in kindness toward us in Christ Jesus that He has promised to us in the ages to come when He makes all things new. AC

Pray it:

READ IT

Day Fifteen: 1 Peter 1:18-19

Write it:

_____

_____

_____

_____

_____

Ponder it:

Legacy and family heritage can be good things but boy, they sure can be nasty too. It's true that we are our mom's daughters and our father's sons and all of us are recipients of bad legacy- of selfishness, generational strongholds, patterns of sin. But in Christ, we are redeemed from these things. All those generations of alcoholics in your family? The bad blood between brothers past? The drama, the foolishness, the patterns of relationships, the pitfalls and strongholds? You are redeemed from the futile way of life inherited from your forefathers. The deal is sealed, once for all and we are safely delivered from the past. What a gospel. What a Christ! AJ

Pray it:

READ IT

Day Sixteen: Romans 8:10-11

Write it:

Ponder it:

Jesus promised, "I will not leave you as orphans; I will come to you" (John 14:18). And then He sent His Spirit to dwell in the hearts of all who trusted in Him. If the Spirit of Jesus lives within us, we are not fatherless orphans, wandering aimlessly, timidly hoping that God might possibly remember to send us some distant celestial comfort, but we are adopted sons of God, heirs alongside the One whose Spirit we carry within our bodies. His glory resides within our weary, sin-riddled flesh, and we are alive because of the righteousness of the One whose Spirit we bear. Since Jesus has left us with the staggering down-payment of His very Spirit within us, our coming inheritance is as sure as the seal of the Spirit on our hearts. What is future to us is already as good as done in God's mind. By faith we persevere in hope, crying out "Abba! Father!" through the One who promises never to leave or forsake us. Very soon our eyes will see that eternal weight of glory for which we long and to which our redeemed souls are destined. AC

Pray it:

READ IT

Day Seventeen: 1 John 4:10

Write it:

_____

_____

_____

_____

_____

Ponder it:

It's a strange word, propitiation. Not your everyday slang. So let's do some imagining to understand it. Imagine God is a perfect God (He is), that He is just (He is) and cannot allow the slightest wrongdoing to go unpunished (He can't). Now imagine He is carrying out perfect justice and punishment for sin, person by person, one at a time and His eyes just turned to you. You're up. In one glance, He knows your every failure, fault, hidden sin, and deeply depraved thought. And it's judgment time. Imagine the wrath and judgment of God due you come hurtling your way, perfectly measured and suitable for your every sin. There is no running, no escaping, no hiding. You are hopeless. But wait. Imagine something, Someone, stepping in front of you in the nick of time, coming between you and Judgment, shielding you from God's wrath and absorbing the full measure of God's anger poured out and meant for you, down to the very last drop. That's propitiation. Christ as propitiation means Christ absorbed all God's wrath that was poured out to punish our sin. The outcome is the complete satisfaction of God. He is appeased. We are atoned for by the death of God's very own Son and are forever at peace with God. Propitiation. What a glorious word. AJ

Pray it:

READ IT

Day Eighteen: Romans 5:12-21

Write it:

_____

_____

_____

_____

_____

Ponder it:

Ever since that fateful, horrible day when sin entered into the world, we have lived under the reign of death caused by Adam's disobedience. Every single soul conceived is a member of Adam's family tree, suffering the consequences God had promised for sin: "You shall surely die." The ramifications of Adam's sin have been far-reaching, eternal, and horrible. All of us are born under the headship of our natural father, Adam, but even before the beginning of time, God planned to send a second Adam in the person of His Son, Jesus. For us who have received the good news—the gospel that says Jesus is the promised Redeemer who died for sinners, was buried, and is now alive again—we are born again into Christ. For as in Adam all die, so also in Christ shall all be made alive, a great hope for us who have been adopted into a new family tree, the family tree of Jesus. And just as we have borne the image of Adam, the man of dust, we shall also bear the image of Jesus, the man of heaven. AC

Pray it:

READ IT

Day Nineteen: Romans 6:11-13

Write it:

_____

_____

_____

_____

_____

Ponder it:

The way you think about yourself matters. After all, Christ purchased a brand new identity for you. We must begin to think about ourselves as someone "in Christ." There are two core truths about being in Christ. 1. You are dead to sin. A dead person is non-responsive. It doesn't matter if you threaten, beg, plead, even torture, you will get no response from them. In regards to sin, you are dead. 2. You are alive to God. You are quickened to the things of God, tuned into righteousness, able to choose what pleases Him. We are not spiritual invalids, stuck in some spiritual wheelchair and un-capable of doing what's right. We need to know it, think it, believe it, and act on it: we are dead to sin and alive unto God! AJ

Pray it:

READ IT

Day Twenty: Ephesians 2:4-5, Romans 6:11

Write it:

_____

_____

_____

_____

_____

Ponder it:

Marching in step under the banner of our father the devil, we waved our flags of rebellion and set ourselves against the Lord and His Son, King Jesus. "BUT GOD...made us alive together with Christ." A God rich in mercy, the Son's blood that He shed on our behalf was the purchase price to redeem us to Himself, we are a people called out from behind enemy lines. One would scarcely die for a good person, but God demonstrates His love for us in that He sent His Son to die for the spiritually dead souls who hated Him. Even while we were sinners, He made us alive together with His Son, an act that was a miracle and an outrageous gift. Now that our souls have been quickened alive by His life-giving Spirit, we must reckon ourselves dead to sin and alive to God in Christ Jesus. This means that, as we walk in the good works which God prepared beforehand for us, we present our bodies to God as instruments of righteousness, acknowledging and acting upon the truth that we have been brought from death to life and from the dominion of Satan to the kingdom of God's beloved Son. AC

Pray it:

READ IT

Day Twenty-one: 1 Timothy 1:15

Write it:

Ponder it:

The pre-requisite for salvation is being a sinner. You don't need to be worthy. You don't have to be lovable. You don't need to be popular, proven, or liked by anyone, not even yourself. None of those things are required. The only requirement is that you be a sinner who exercises faith in a God good enough to die for the likes of you. See what great news that is? Not only is this news amazing, it is also reliable and totally trustworthy. We can place the weight of our souls, sin and all our eternity on this one truth: Jesus Christ came to save sinners. And I qualify! AJ

Pray it:

READ IT

Day Twenty-two: Romans 5:1

Write it:

Ponder it:

Although we deserve the wrath of God's righteous anger against sin, God poured out all of His holy fury onto His sinless Son, the Lord Jesus. Three days later, He raised Him from the dead, a powerful display of the finished work of Christ Jesus on the cross. The resurrection demonstrates that God's wrath against sin is completely, totally quenched in the vengeance He exacted upon His own Son. Now, God's full favor and delight rest upon His Son whom He raised from the dead. For all of us who receive God's great, free gift of the sacrifice of His Son on our behalf, we are justified, a legal term that declares us righteous in the sight of a holy God. Just as God finds full pleasure in smiling upon His risen Son, for us who are "in Christ," the full favor of God rests upon us, too. Because of the work of Jesus on our behalf, God says to the forgiven sinner, "There is now peace between Me and you. Case dismissed." AC

Pray it:

READ IT

Day Twenty-three: Hebrews 9:14

Write it:

Ponder it:

Conscience, settle down. Yes, you are right that I am a sinner. I've blown it. I failed miserably. But the blood of Jesus has atoned for that thing you are so intent on reminding me of. The Judge Himself says no one can bring a charge against me, not even you. The charges have been brought before Him and nailed to the cross. He has acquitted me, on the basis of Another. So be cleansed conscience! Be cleansed by the Blood of Christ. AJ

Pray it:

READ IT

Day Twenty-four: 1 Peter 1:3-4

Write it:

_____

_____

_____

_____

_____

Ponder it:

For the Christian, all of our future hope hangs upon the resurrection of Jesus Christ that followed his sacrificial death. By looking with pleading eyes of faith to the mercy offered upon the cross, we are born again, a new creation in Christ Jesus. But without the resurrection, dead people cannot be raised and sinners have no hope of a living Savior. But in fact, Christ has been raised from the dead! He is the "first fruits" of all the born again souls, those cleansed by His blood. What a glorious new life we have been born into, and what joy and glory await us! Because of our Savior's resurrection, we rejoice with joy that is inexpressible and filled with glory as we await our future inheritance that is kept by God who promises that the final outcome of our faith is the ultimate salvation of our souls and the obtaining of the inheritance that is ours in our new birth because of the resurrection power of His Son. AC

Pray it:

READ IT

Day Twenty-five: 2 Corinthians 3:18

Write it:

_____

_____

_____

_____

_____

Ponder it:

As much as we like the idea of instantaneous goodness, of a mountain top experience that fixes us once and for all, Scripture doesn't promise us this type of sanctification. It does, however, promise us transformation. "We are being transformed!" How? By gazing upon the glory of Christ. It wasn't with riches, honor, and slick marketing that Christ showed us His glory, but with His humility. He humbled Himself to the point of death, even death on the cross. As we consider the humble, sacrificial love of our Redeemer, we are transformed. The way up is down. The greatest is the servant. And it is not through

our own striving and trying harder that we are transformed, but through considering the One who showed us
true Glory. AJ

Pray it:

READ IT

Day Twenty-six: Romans 15:7

Write it:

Ponder it:

How was it that Christ welcomed us? Did He welcome us in our penitence and humility? Did He welcome us because we were pleasant, obedient, and perfect? No, but He welcomed us in our weakness, in our sinful state, in our rebellion. He passed over our sins because of the soul-cleansing nature of His blood, and He received us to Himself for the glory of God. As we have freely received, now by the power of the Spirit that He has lavished upon our hearts, we freely give acceptance and love, just like our Savior and Head, King Jesus. He is the God of endurance and encouragement, and by following in His steps and welcoming the weak, we model the Gospel to the sick and sinful, the needy and despised, the dirty and helpless, taking them to ourselves in warm embrace. Because of the great love and humility of Christ toward us in our sin, we can take no thought for pleasing ourselves, but we can bear with the weak, one beggar telling another beggar where to find bread. AC

Pray it:

READ IT

Day Twenty-seven: Romans 8:33-34

Write it:

_____

_____

_____

_____

_____

Ponder it:

The Double Jeopardy Clause is a legal provision that says a person cannot be charged with the same crime twice. Once someone has been tried and either acquitted or charged with a crime, that person cannot be called into court and prosecuted again for that offense. One of the reasons this provision exists is to uphold the finality and integrity of the court. Likewise, the finality and integrity of Christ's work means no one can bring a charge against you again, not even your own conscience. All charges have been brought and the trial is over. God has justified and no one can condemn... forever. AJ

Pray it:

READ IT

Day Twenty-eight: Isaiah 53:4-6

Write it:

_____

_____

_____

_____

_____

Ponder it:

The innocent One suffered as my substitute: He bore my griefs and He carried my sorrows. God the Father severely punished God the Son for my sin, piercing Him, crushing Him, chastising Him, wounding Him. Fulfilling the promise He made in the Garden, God provided a sacrifice for sin, a Lamb to be crushed as an offering for my guilt. That sacrifice was the offering up of His only Son. I am the wayward one, but upon the perfect sinless One, God laid all of my sin. The sin-bearing, spotless Lamb of God laid down His life, and He bore my shame when the record of my guilt was placed upon Him, His flesh receiving the nails while His blood poured out from His sword-pierced side and thorn-crowned brow. The Holy God, dwelling in inapproachable light, saw the anguish of His soul, and He was satisfied with the offering that was made for my sin. "Full atonement!" Can it be? Hallelujah! What a Savior! AC

Pray it:

READ IT

Day Twenty-nine: Romans 4:5

Write it:

Ponder it:

So you yelled at the kids. You brushed them off when they needed your attention, wasted time on the Internet, gave your husband the cold shoulder, and borrowed bill money to buy pizza because you didn't feel like cooking dinner. The accuser of the brethren is having a heyday with all those failures and is hounding you about what a loser you are, how you don't hold a light to so and so, how much you should be ashamed of yourself, and on and on. Enter one little gospel word: "justified." Justification says God considers you righteous because of the work of Jesus Christ. Therefore, you can preach the gospel to yourself like this: "Who will bring a charge against God's elect? God is the one who justifies (Romans 8:33). Yes, I have sinned today. I have been selfish and lazy and rude and wasteful. I have failed to keep God's moral law and failed to love my family. Nevertheless, God's Word says that God justifies the ungodly (Romans 4:5), apart from works of the law (Romans 3:21). God justifies the one who places her faith in the work of Jesus Christ. I therefore, in simple trust, cast myself upon the work of Christ and the provision of the cross as my only hope. I receive the gift of God and trust that in spite of my sin, I have been justified by faith and am at peace with God (Romans 5:1)." And you can go to bed happy and joyful and pure of heart knowing your sin has been taken care of in Christ. AJ

Pray it:

READ IT

Day Thirty: Ephesians 1:5, John 1:12

Write it:

_____

_____

_____

_____

_____

Ponder it:

When the man Nicodemus, who was a teacher and ruler in Israel, asked Jesus how it could be that a grown man could be born again in order to see the kingdom of God, Nicodemus pictured a child being grown in the womb of a pregnant woman and then being born into her family. Jesus explained to him that men and women do not need to be physically born again, but that anyone who would see the kingdom of God must be born of the Spirit. How does this Spirit-birth into the family of God take place? When anyone believes in God's only Son, he or she is born again to a new eternal, spiritual life, not by physical birth, but by spiritual adoption. All who are led by the Spirit of God are sons and daughters of God, and by faith in Jesus, we have received the Spirit of adoption, by whom we cry, "Abba! Father!" AC

Pray it:

READ IT

Day Thirty-one: 1 Thessalonians 5:9

Write it:

_____

_____

_____

_____

_____

Ponder it:

Sin and shame can hound a soul like the bitterness of
winter can the bones. They can remind us of what we're
good and worthy of: judgment. Our value can be tied to
our behavior, our sin pot-marking and scarring the soul.
We can cringe and cower in our own dark stench. Oh,
and let's not forget the fear sin and shame bring. Oh, how
they make us fear! Yet there is an antidote to fear, sin,
and shame and it's the perfect love of God. This love dri-
ves out fear and reminds us of our destiny: you are not
appointed for stumbling. You are not destined for destruction. You are on the trajectory to eternal life because

of Jesus Christ. You've been snatched from the fires of judgment, set on the path of life, forgiven of your sins and secured by the Spirit. To the sin-sick soul there is but one instruction: get to the cross of Christ. There you will find your eyesight for these things. There you will find healing. There you will find your wondrous destiny. AJ

Pray it:

READ IT

Day Thirty-two: Isaiah 61:10

Write it:

_____

_____

_____

_____

_____

Ponder it:

On my wedding day, I stepped into a white satin dress, covered my head with a sheer veil, and clasped my mother's strand of pearls about my neck. I was ready to meet my beloved husband and enter into our marriage through a ceremony and a great feast that was prepared for our guests. That beautiful wedding day was a wispy shadow of a great day coming, when the bride of Christ will meet her Groom, and she will be dressed in the righteousness purchased for her by Him. No one dressed in the filthy rags of their own righteousness will be at that marriage supper of the Lamb, but only those who have put on the righteousness of Christ, the garments of salvation by which the bride is adorned for her Husband. Rejoice in the Lord! Exult in your God, o church! For He has made His bride ready. Blessed are those who are invited to the marriage supper of the Lamb! AC

Pray it:

READ IT

Day Thirty-three: 1 Peter 2:8b-10

Write it:

_____

_____

_____

_____

_____

Ponder it:

Chosen. Royal. Holy. God's very own treasure. These terms describe what you are, your truest identity. Yet look closely and you will find something else just as wondrous: your purpose. You possess a high calling, a worthy pursuit, a life mission. You are an enlisted man or woman, on a mission to proclaim excellent things regarding your wondrous King. You are a minister of the gospel, an ambassador for Christ, a servant of the Most High God. You've been entrusted with the ministry of reconciliation and your feet bear tidings of good news. You are the aroma of Christ wherever you go. You are set apart for a glorious calling as a chosen race...a royal priesthood...a holy nation. Now go fulfill your calling. AJ

Pray it:

READ IT

Day Thirty-four: Acts 13:38-39

Write it:

_____

_____

_____

_____

_____

Ponder it:

We stumble when we attempt to bear upon our shoulders the weight of keeping The Law or place its yoke around the necks of our children to be obeyed. The Law is good and right, displaying God's impeccable, impossible standard of perfection, but we are under a curse if we rely on works of the Law to be justified in God's sight, for we are cursed if we do not abide by all things written within it. But by believing in Jesus, the One who redeemed us from the curse of the Law by hanging on a cross to become a curse for us, we are made truly free, justified before God through the forgiveness offered to us by faith in Christ. So then, indulging our flesh and yielding to the temptation to seek our freedom through our own righteous works or motives leads to imprisonment, but receiving the free gift of forgiveness of sins offered in Jesus liberates us from every chain and weight that only He can lift from our weary shoulders and our sinful hearts. AC

Pray it:

READ IT

Day Thirty-five: Hebrews 10:10,14; 7:25

Write it:

Ponder it:

"Once for all." "For all time." "Forever." These words reassure us our God is capable of fully and single handedly handling our salvation. The blood of Christ is sufficient. Jesus offered one sacrifice for sins for all time (Hebrews 10:12) and our part is to stand in full assurance of faith (Hebrews 10:22). That's it! We are not the heroes of this story. We do not need to muster some measure- any measure- of righteousness up for our own sanctification. Christ is the end of the law to all who believe! (Romans 4:4) Soul, stop seeking to establish your own right-eousness. Subject yourself to the righteousness of God, the righteousness of faith (Romans 4:3). Do not throw away your confidence in the Savior who has perfected you once for all. AJ

Pray it:

READ IT

Day Thirty-six: Colossians 1:13

Write it:

_____

_____

_____

_____

_____

Ponder it:

God redeemed us for Himself by the forgiveness of our sins in Christ, and with us He is building for Himself a kingdom. In His holy wisdom, not many of the ones He is calling to Himself are the mighty, the wise, the power-ful, or the noble, but He is choosing those who are low, despised, and weak to grow His kingdom. From those who are nothing, He is calling out a kingdom of people for His own possession, that we may proclaim the excel-lencies of Him who called us out of darkness and into His marvelous light. Once, we were nobodies, aimless and shackled enemies of God, without hope or mercy, but

God made us His people, His kingdom, His own holy nation. He chose us and qualified us for His kingdom through the purchase price of our redemption through His Son, and because the Architect and Builder of this holy kingdom is the LORD, we are bold and sure that the gates of hell shall not prevail against it. AC

Pray it:

READ IT

Day Thirty-seven: Romans 5:8

Write it:

_____

_____

_____

_____

_____

Ponder it:

What comfort and hope we find in knowing that God gave His Son for our sins while we were still His enemies! If we ever doubt His love or wonder if His care for us has faltered, we look to the sacrifice of Jesus on our behalf, and we see demonstrated the deep love of God for us, long before we loved Him. Not only can we rest with great confidence in His love for us, but we are also assured that, if God gave His Son to justify us by His blood while we were still His enemies, then we are all the more confident that He will not forsake us or forget us now that His Son lives forever to make intercession for us! He will bring us into His glory and rescue us on the day of His wrath. And so we take great joy in God through our Lord Jesus Christ, since because of the gift of His Son, we who once were God's enemies are now those whom He claims as His friends. AC

Pray it:

READ IT

Day Thirty-eight: Jude 24-25

Write it:

Ponder it:

Against the black backdrop of our sin, the diamond of the gospel shines its brightest. This good news is of One "able to keep us from stumbling." He is sufficient; capable; able. He not only forgives us our past sins but is able to keep us from stumbling in the present and future as well. When we've come to the end of our resources and fallen short of the glory of God (yet again), we can trust in the ability of our Savior. The Person and work of Christ is able to make us stand faultless before our God, now and forevermore. We will one day stand in His presence with great joy. There will be no shame. No guilt. No regret. Just joy. Only One Savior can do that and to Him belongs all glory, majesty, dominion, and authority, from eternity past to eternity future! AJ

Pray it:

READ IT

Day Thirty-nine: 1 John 4:18

Write it:

_____

_____

_____

_____

_____

Ponder it:

Oh, that God would give us strength to comprehend what is the breadth and length and height and depth of Christ's love for us. May we know that love that surpasses knowledge, because knowing God's love for us through His Son unlocks chains of fear and lifts griefs of doubt that weigh down our hearts. What depths of peace we find when we learn to soothe our souls to the tune of "Jesus loves me, this I know, for the Bible tells me so." Our fears are stilled, all strivings cease, and we stand secure in God's love, made manifest to us when God sent His only Son into the world, so that we might live through Him. There is a great day of judgment coming, but God's love was demonstrated by sending His Son as the propitiation -- the atoning sacrifice -- for our sins. And so, for those who have the Son, we have an Advocate with the Father, Jesus Christ the righteous. In the face of judgment and punishment, we will not be ashamed, because the love that we now believe through eyes of faith and hearts of hope, we then will see face to face. AC

Pray it:

READ IT

Day Forty: Luke 22:19-20

Write it:

Ponder it:

For forty days our hearts have burned within us as we've considered the work of Christ and the provisions of the cross. We've nourished ourselves with the grace gifts of justification, transformation, forgiveness, redemption, adoption, and unconditional love. How fitting that on this final day we hear the words—yes, the very heart—of Christ Himself. "This is My body which is given for you. This is My blood, poured out for you." Christ knew the personal cost He would pay for our redemption. But He also knew what His death would accomplish on our behalf. Christ says to you, "This is given for you." For you. YOU. Can you hear His voice speaking? Can you hear His love calling? It was for you. Given freely and generously, He invites us to feast on His broken body and His life-blood that purchased for us the very blessing of God. Worthy is the Lamb that was slain! As we partake of communion, may we, the bride of Christ, remember His gift and freely give to Him all power and wealth and wisdom and strength and honor and glory and praise. Worthy is the Lamb! AJ

Pray it:

Made in the USA
Columbia, SC
28 May 2020